G

CORNWALL

Dedicated to Helen, Sam and Garth
whose love and understanding made the
early mornings and late evenings bearable.

CORNWALL

Photographed by

Richard Strong

With a Foreword by

Tim Smit

Text by

Chris Robinson

MABECRON BOOKS

THE NATIONAL TRUST

Much of the coastal landscape and many of the houses and gardens that feature in "Cornwall" are owned and permanently protected by the National Trust. The publishers are deeply grateful to the Trust for its co-operation in the production of this book, which vividly highlights the rôle of the Trust in caring for the best of Cornwall.

914.37

N

Perranporth ●

St Agnes ●

Porthtowan ●

Godrevy
Lighthouse

St Ives ●   Redruth ●
           ●
                    Camborne ●

Zennor ●

● Hayle

Cape Cornwall ●   Penzance
                            ● St Michael's Mount
           Newlyn ●   ●
Sennen Cove ●   ● Prussia Cove
                        ● Mousehole

Porthcurno
●

Mullion ●

Kynance Cove ●
                              ●
Lizard Point

● Isles of Scilly

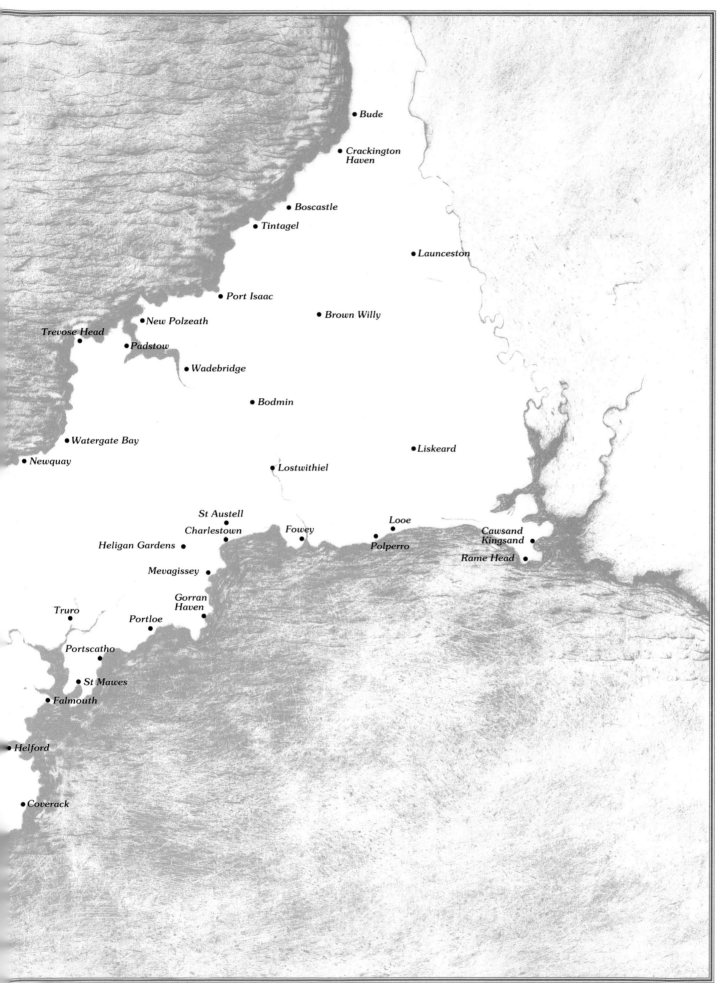

Bude

Crackington
Haven

Boscastle

Tintagel

Launceston

Port Isaac

New Polzeath

Brown Willy

Trevose Head

Padstow

Wadebridge

Bodmin

Watergate Bay

Liskeard

Newquay

Lostwithiel

St Austell

Looe

Charlestown

Fowey

Cawsand
Kingsand

Heligan Gardens

Polperro

Rame Head

Mevagissey

Gorran
Haven

Truro

Portloe

Portscatho

St Mawes

Falmouth

Helford

Coverack

Map drawn by Katrina Cook

Foreword

To live in Cornwall is a privilege. Its fiercely independent people, untamed even by the Romans, maintain a way of life and sense of community that the many newcomers who have chosen to live here over the passing years have failed to dilute. I well recall the day in 1990 when we discovered the "Thunderbox Room" among the derelict former working buildings at Heligan. Etched in pencil on the flaky plaster wall, a motto, "come ye not here to sleep nor slumber". Underneath, the gardeners had signed their names. The date August 1914. The outbreak of the Great War. The next time we came across most of them was on the memorial cross in St Ewe churchyard. Every one of those names is still represented in the local community. There are not many places of which that can be said.

Two thousand years have passed since the Phoenicians first plied their trade here. Today, the tin mines, whose skeletal remains form a recurring and brooding backdrop to the Cornish landscape, are passing into proud history. The prehistoric tombs and iron age hill forts attest to an older history that accounts for the romantic notions of ghosts that walk this land of mists, and whose very wildness was the stuff of legends.

As with all the Celtic races the Cornish have had to put up with the jibes others, at once suspicious and frightened of their differences, have hurled at them. The Cornish for their part have never made the mistake of confusing blandness for sophistication. One only has to see the passions of Trelawney's army unleashed on rugby days to realise that this is some other place.

Cornwall's uniquely mild climate led to the creation of gardens whose spectacular living theatre has rightly been celebrated across the world, yet this climate once also gave us an agricultural advantage that the global market, with its disregard for seasons, has now undermined.

The sea which once shaped the lives of thousands who made a hard living from harvesting its bounty, is meaner in its favours now. The picturesque communities that nurtured them are more likely earning their livings from the visitors than the fishing. Why do they come in their thousands? It's my belief they have come in search of something they lost many years ago – a spirit of place and a sense of belonging.

The Cornish have a saying that is at once hopeful and threatening; "the tide comes in twice a day". As the communications industry comes of age and the magnetic pull of the city loses many of its attractions, one can be at the heart of events wherever you are. Something is stirring in this land and I feel that the tide is turning.

The South

Tamar Bridges

The two classic suspension bridges crossing the Tamar at Saltash are the lowest fixed crossing points between Devon and Cornwall. Brunel's bridge to the left gave Cornwall the earliest access for rail travellers in the mid-nineteenth century. Still the only rail link it stands next to the modern road bridge as a unique example of architectural engineering.

River Lynher

Mount Edgcumbe

In recent years the eighth Earl of Mount Edgcumbe has handed the running of the magnificent Mount Edgcumbe estate over to Caradon County Council and Plymouth City Council. The park and extensive grounds are now open to the public all year round. The house was first built in the middle of the sixteenth century after Sir Piers Edgcumbe moved the family seat here from Cotehele. Elaborately altered and extended in the seventeenth century the house was gutted during the air raids on Plymouth in the Second World War and was later reconstructed along the lines of the original plans of the 1540s.

Gates at Mount Edgcumbe

Cawsand Bay

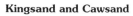

Kingsand and Cawsand

The secluded villages of Kingsand and Cawsand lie tucked away on the eastern side of the Rame Peninsula.

Their timeless tranquillity is protected by their relative isolation from the county's main road system.

Rame Chapel, Rame Head

Rame Chapel sits at the very tip of the Rame Peninsula on the top of the exposed headland you see in the picture on the right. It offers uninterrupted views of water in almost every direction. In the past it fulfilled the dual functions of both a place of prayer for those at sea and a place where a light burned to guide passing seafarers. Dedicated to St Michael in 1397, this early lighthouse is now a ruin – a number of other chapels in elevated locations are also associated with St Michael.

Rame Church, Rame Head

Dedicated to St German and built of rough slate, Rame Church was constructed principally around its thirteenth century nave and chancel and has been little altered since the fifteenth century.

Whitsand Bay
looking across
to Rame Head

Restormel Castle

Restormel Castle stands sentinel on a sculptured hill top near the river Fowey and above the town of Lostwithiel. Constructed in the Middle ages it is regarded as one of Cornwall's most impressive examples of military architecture.

Portwrinkle
The small village of Portwrinkle is nestled on the coastline between Rame Head and Looe. Better known for the nearby golf course the beach is always popular with families and dog lovers.

Looking west from Portwrinkle

On the Beach
Portwrinkle

A gig entering Looe Harbour at sunset
The number of working fishing boats here help to create Looe's character. It is a popular base for shark fishermen, and as the sun sets, its narrow streets glow with the soft lights of restaurants, pubs and gift shops that now do so much to contribute to its character.

Banjo Pier, Looe Harbour
In some respects, the sun set over Banjo Pier, East Looe, many years ago. In its heyday, the harbour was a centre of considerable commercial activity. Ore was shipped to be smelted and a great deal of fish landed. Looe was also a victualling station for the Royal Navy.

Liskeard Viaduct

When trains eventually made their way into Cornwall in the 1860s, it was quite apparent that the undulating countryside was never going to be the easiest to traverse. Hence the number of impressive viaducts to be seen in the county. It was the very hills that created the obstacles that provided the stone the engineers needed to overcome the problem.

Polperro

Polperro, with its mix of white washed and pastel painted cottages, its higgledy-piggledy streets, the stream running through this deep-cut, green wooded valley, the house on stilts and its double harbour which opens onto the rugged Cornish coast, all conspire to make Polperro one of the most charming and frequently visited fishing villages in the county.

Lerryn Water

One hundred years ago Arthur Norway wrote of Lerryn Creek in his ***Highways and Byways of Cornwall:***

"The beautiful creek of Lerrin lies behind us, the church of St Winnow, so finely placed on the very margin of the river drifts slowly past and is hidden by its woods, and now the country opens into level water meadows, and a little way ahead the spire of Lostwithiel church stands out among the lower hills… At this point we touch the loveliest inland scenery in Cornwall."

St Winnow Church

Pasture at Lerryn

Bodinnick Ferry, Fowey
Fowey takes its name from
the river which flows through
it, rising on Bodmin Moor.
The name is thought to
derive from the beech trees
that stand beside the river.
Looking out for many years
on this particular stretch of
the river was the author
Daphne Du Maurier who
lived in the house seen here
on the right. She wrote
Rebecca here in 1938,
and only left in 1967 when
the Rashleighs reclaimed
their house.

Messing about in boats
Kenneth Grahame, was a
regular visitor to the town.
Fowey is said to have inspired
much of *The Wind in the
Willows* river setting for
"messing about in boats".

Lanhydrock House

Lanhydrock

One of a number of fine National Trust properties in Cornwall, the Lanhydrock estate was bought by Sir Richard Robartes, a wealthy Truro tin and wool merchant, in 1620. Some forty-nine rooms are currently open to the public, but not all are seventeenth century as a large part of the house was rebuilt after a major fire in 1881. Beautifully situated above the River Fowey south of Bodmin the extensive gardens are a delight at any time of year.

33

Clay

The most recent of major extractive industries to bring money into Cornwall is also the one which has probably had the biggest visual impact on the county. Few find the great white tips and troughs of the clay business pleasing to the eye. China Clay is the product of "kaolinisation" – the action of rainwater on granite fuelled by residual heat of the rocks over millions of years. The deposits are concentrated around the villages to the north of St Austell and it is there that the effects of the industry are most striking.

Autumn woods

Winter woods

Charlestown Harbour

Conceived by Charles Rashleigh (hence Charlestown), it was carved out in the 1790s when, what had been the tiny community of Polmear was transformed into a bustling harbour shipping tin, copper and especially china clay. Today, television and film crews regularly make use of its period charm.

Mevagissey Harbour

Mevagissey

Mevagissey is one of Cornwall's oldest fishing villages. It was a leading pilchard fishery in Tudor times, however, the fisherman's catch today is much more diverse. The charming inner harbour and the narrow streets are a hive of activity in the summer months and a pleasure to wander around on a fine evening.

The Gardens at Heligan
The Lost Gardens of
Heligan have become one
of Cornwall's most popular
attractions. The gardens
have evolved since the late
eighteenth century, and
contain plants from all over
the world. The estate fell
into neglect during the First
World War when members
of the family and the
gardeners failed to return
from the Front. However
the decades of neglect
allowed the more interesting
flora to thrive under a
blanket of brambles. The
recent restoration of the
'jungle', the Italian garden,
the walled garden and the
many others have returned
the gardens to a state their
architect would have
recognised, and has
encouraged thousands of
people to visit Heligan in
the process.

Gorran Haven

Gorran Haven is a comparatively recent name for this village. Until the late eighteenth century it was known as Port-East, before this it was known as Porthjust. It was described in the 1830s as "a small port… supposed to have been anciently of more consequence". During the nineteenth century coal was imported through the port, and great quantities of pilchard were landed and cured. Today it is a popular summer resort for holiday-makers staying in the area.

The Beach at Gorran Haven

**Looking across Gerrans
Bay to Nare Head**

Portloe

Portloe, which means 'harbour of an inlet' or 'inlet cove', is one of those delightful tiny fishing communities that hasn't changed much in years. The little stream that flows down to the cove has long been built over and now flows on to the beach beneath the seventeenth century Lugger Hotel.

St Mawes

At the end of the Roseland
peninsular, its isolated yet
sheltered position at the
mouth of Carrick Roads,
and ready access to the
open sea makes St Mawes
a favourite for yachtsmen.

St Mawes Castle
The castle was built between 1540 and 1543. Its dominant position was selected to guard Carrick Roads from attack by the French.

St Mawes

Riverside house

King Harry Ferry
Long and winding tree-lined roads on either side of the Fal lead down to the King Harry Ferry. This is the lowest vehicular crossing point of Cornwall's busiest waterway and nowhere is the lush vegetation that surrounds this spot more delightfully displayed than in the gardens of Trelissick on the western bank.

St Just-in-Roseland
The medieval church of St Just-in-Roseland was consecrated in 1261, and stands at the bottom of a woody coombe on the western side of the Roseland peninsular. Take a timeless walk around the churchyard and admire the many flowering shrubs and sub-tropical plants collected from around the world in the nineteenth century by John Garland Trevender. The name 'Roseland' comes from the Cornish 'ros' meaning a promontory.

Sailing on the Fal

Truro by night

Truro

Truro is the present day administrative centre of Cornwall. The city's most prominent landmark is the huge nineteenth century cathedral. Although the cathedral is quite modern there are hints of Truro's history in the honey-coloured Georgian houses in Lemon street, built by the local merchant William Lemon. At the top of the hill stands a statue of Richard Lander the first holder of the Royal Geographical Society's Gold Medal.

Trelissick Gardens

The beautiful gardens of Trelissick were laid out in the 1820's with spectacular views across the river Fal and Carrick Roads. The main feature of the gardens is the plentiful array of camellias, magnolias and hydrangeas and sub-tropical species from South America and Tasmania. Now owned by the National Trust the gardens are occasionally used for plays and concerts in the summer months.

Overleaf:
Upper reaches of the Fal.

Pendennis Castle

The name 'Pendennis', translated literally, means 'the headland of a fortific-ation', which probably referred to an iron-age fort lost in the building of the Castle. Pendennis was completed in 1546 by King Henry VIII, it is now managed by English Heritage and attracts a great many visitors each year.

The waterfront at Falmouth

Falmouth Docks

Sitting at the mouth of the Fal, Falmouth Harbour is the busiest port in Cornwall, and is capable of handling vessels of up to 100,000 tons. It is the third deepest natural harbour in the world. Its true potential was realised by Sir Walter Raleigh and by Sir John Killigrew who lived nearby at Arwennack Manor, together they were responsible for transforming a fishing village into an emergent new town. Falmouth was granted its own Charter in 1661. It continues to prosper to this day.

The West

Helford from the air
Looking along the Helford
river we see a large unspoilt
'ria' that is a drowned valley.
Its many creeks and woods
have retained their natural
appearance. To the west
of the village of Helford,
below the daffodil fields, is
'Frenchmans Creek' made
famous in Daphne Du
Maurier's novel. The river is
rich with flora and fauna
especially its oyster beds and
heronries.

Glendurgan

Although possessed of many fine trees, rare and exotic plants and delightful water gardens, the undoubted highlight of Glendurgan Gardens is the recently restored laurel maze which was first laid out in 1833. However, perhaps even more of a curiosity is the charming little group of cottages that make up the tiny hamlet of Durgan itself, which sits at the water's edge at the very bottom of this picturesque valley garden.

Glendurgan Gardens

Trebah

Like neighbouring Glendurgan, Trebah Gardens stretch down to the mouth of the Helford River. First planted over 150 years ago the delightful, mature collection of flora is set around a meandering stream which cascades down to a large pool, reaching the river across a small south-facing pebbly beach in Polgwidden Cove. Spectacular hydrangeas, rhodedendrons and magnolias provide a blaze of colour against an exotic backdrop of large leafed plants, palms and a wide variety of ferns.

Coverack morning

Coverack at evening

The mist starts to settle over the fishing and former smuggling community of Coverack. A safe landing place for those who know it well, it had a different reputation when ship's navigation equipment was somewhat less advanced than it is today, for just a mile or so to the east are the Manacles. This group of sea swept rocks have brought many a boat to grief and have twice claimed more than a hundred lives.

Cadgwith

With no man-made harbour, the great attraction of the small yet picturesque port of Cadgwith is that the fishing boats which work out of here are beached in such a way that the visitor can see a catch being brought in at close quarters.

Kynance Cove

On the beach

Kynance

A true wonder of nature, you cannot fail to be moved by the almost cathedral-like quality of the water-drilled caves and the sea-beaten serpentine rocks that stand firm in the golden sand of Kynance. Each has its own distinctive character and each has its own name – there's Bishop, the Bellows, the Letter Box, the Man O'War, Sugarloaf Rock and Asparagus Island. The caves too have distinctive, if not rather domestic, names – the Kitchen, the Parlour and the Dressing Room.

Serpentine on the Lizard

The southernmost point of England is a dramatic place, its distinctive serpentine rock fashioned into rugged cliffs. Treacherous for generations of sea-farers, the Lizard has been a safer place since Sir John Killigrew, of Falmouth, had a lighthouse built here in the first half of the seventeenth century. Since modified and updated the former coal burning light now throws an electric beam some 20 miles across the sea.

The Lizard Lighthouse

Mullion Cove

Mullion Cove, late afternoon, the seagulls wheeling around the boat full of divers. There was once a busy fishing community here, the great stone jetties were constructed to shelter the men and their boats in the late-nineteenth century. Mullion itself and the church, complete with its famous sixteenth century bench end carvings, is a mile or so up the road.

St Michael's Mount

St Michael's Mount stands some four hundred yards out from Marazion and is negotiable by means of a stone causeway at low tide. The spectacular natural setting has made it an important habitat through the ages. Historically it has been claimed as Ictis, the island used in the Phoenician tin trade thousands of years ago, the Romans are also said to have used it and the British virgin St Keyne is said to have made a pilgrimage here 1600 years ago. Until the dissolution of the monasteries it served for several centuries as a religious base but since the late-seventeenth century it has been the family seat of the St Aubyn family. In 1954 the Mount was given to the National Trust and opened to the public. Lord St Aubyn still lives there today.

Prussia Cove

Scillonian

Half an hour before sailing, either from Penzance or St Mary's, the Scillonian III sounds her distinct siren to announce her impending departure. Built in 1977, the one-thousand-ton ferry carries up to 600 passengers each time it makes the 42 mile, $2^1/_2$ hour crossing to and from the Isles of Scilly. An on-board exhibition of maps, photographs and pictures prepares the visitor for the sub-tropical treasures ahead and acquaints the curious with many tales of wrecks around the fifty or so islands – all but a handful of which are uninhabited.

Penzance

Cornwall is not overly blessed with statues and this impressive monument to Sir Humphry Davy, in Penzance, at the top of Market Jew Street, is one of the finest. Davy was born not far from this spot in 1778, and very soon proved himself to be an exceptional scientist and philosopher. He was instrumental in the setting up of the Zoological Society in London in the 1820's and his pioneering experiments set Faraday on his way, but he is perhaps best remembered for his miner's safety lamp, which he is depicted holding.

Newlyn

Newlyn is the home of Cornwall's largest fishing fleet. It is also known because of the group of painters who came to the area at the turn of the century. They captured the essence of the place and its people and became known as the 'Newlyn School' of painters of whom Stanhope Forbes is the most famous.

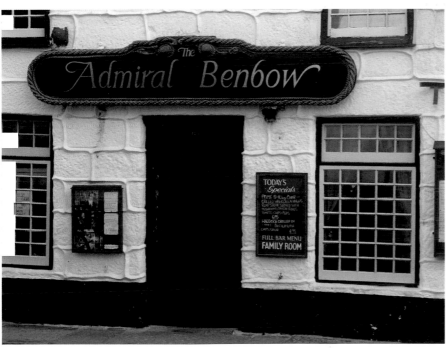

Admiral Benbow

Ship-shape and teeming with nautical artifacts, the busy interior of the Admiral Benbow free house and restaurant is a major Penzance attraction in its own right. It stands on the southern side of Chapel Street, just across from the Maritime Museum. Unassuming from the outside, the museum also sports a ship-shaped arrangement internally, housing a large number of fascinating items rescued by divers from the many old wrecks off the local coastline.

Mousehole

One of the least changed Cornish villages, its 'mousehole' being the small entrance to the harbour. Generations have come to know the village as the home of the Mousehole Cat – Antonia Barber's book, beautifully illustrated by Nicola Bayley about Mowzer the cat and Tom the fisherman. Incidentally, 23rd December in Mousehole is traditionally celebrated as Tom Bawcock's eve. Tom was a fisherman who set out in terrible conditions and, against all the odds, returned with a huge catch to end the famine in the village. The traditional Cornish fish dish Star-gazy Pie is said to commemorate the feast that followed.

Lamorna

Popular with poets, potters, artists and authors, the romantically set, lush green Lamorna Valley ends with the grey quarry-by-the-sea that is Lamorna Cove.

Merry Maidens

The mysteries of Cornish folklore are seldom better evoked than by this enigmatic stone circle near St Buryan. One of more than twenty stone circles in Cornwall this is one the most famous. Legend has is that here we have nineteen merry maidens who were caught dancing on the Sabbath and who were consequently turned to stone, along with the stone Pipers nearby – the pipers being the equally wicked band who were providing the music for the girls to dance to. The nineteen, lichen-covered granite stones, some almost life-size, others much smaller, stand four-square to the elements in a circle some 20 metres in diameter.

Logan's Rock, Porthcurno

The precariously balanced Logan's Rock sits at the head of the beautiful sweeping bay at Porthcurno. Porthcurno was home to the Cable and Wireless Company up until 1994, from here undersea telegraph cables stretch far across the Atlantic giving us a vital communications link with the rest of the world. On the steep granite cliffs next to the village is the renowned Minack Theatre carved into the rock face. The sparkling ocean giving a breathtaking backdrop to the productions that are performed here all summer long.

Cape Cornwall (right)

The tall chimney, an instantly recognisable reminder of Cornwall's tin mining heritage stands proud, bathed in evening light. A rewarding walk from a nearby car-park puts this imposing location within reach of many visitors. Remarkably it is the only "Cape" in England.

Isles of Scilly

Twenty-eight miles off the coast of mainland Cornwall lie the fifty-five islands which make up the archipelago of the Scillies, or sometimes the 'Fortunate Islands'. 'Fortunate' or 'blessed' because of their striking beauty and unique climate. The temperature variation between night and day is small and some islanders claim to have only two seasons, spring and summer. Their beguiling nature hides a history of maritime misery with over 800 shipwrecks being recorded on the surrounding reefs.

The Isles are a renowned halting place for migrant birds in spring and autumn and is a favourite with birdwatchers, its remote tranquillity providing the ideal atmosphere.

The Isles of Scillies industry has been flower farming for the past 100 years, the picking season starts in October and lasts for six months, but its main income is the visitor who comes to find a place that is just 'different.'

Men-an-tol

Men-an-tol – "stone of the hole" is one of the most enduring and endearing of Cornwall's landmarks. Recently shown as having been a part of a stone circle, the magical visual Neolithic alignment of stone and hole has had all manner of powers conferred upon it over the years. It has been hailed as an astronomical marker, a fertility symbol and even a curer of rickets and scrofula. According to one source children suffering with tuberculosis of the lymphatic glands had to pass, naked through Men-an-tol three times and then have their blood drawn on the grass, three times against the sun ... and then they would be cured.

Lanyon Quoit

One of a handful of late Stone Age early Bronze Age portal dolmens, these tombs, or cromlechs, are generally much bigger than you would imagine, even from a dramatic shot like this. The capstone "a great slab of rock eighteen feet long" is "supported on three other slabs which are just a little too low to allow a man to stand upright beneath it."

91

Zennor

Zennor lies in a little hollow, the church on its furthest slope, a worn grey building that harmonises well with the welter of granite blocks that strew the hillsides. The modest medieval church is dedicated to St Sinar or Senner.

An image of the mermaid of Zennor is carved into a bench end of the chancel seat. She allegedly tempted the churchwarden to go to her beneath the waves at Pendour Cove.

St Ives

One beach, Porthminster, catches the best of the morning sun the other makes the most of evening rays and the sea waves. The Atlantic breakers make Porthmeor one of the most frequently portrayed beaches in Cornwall. St Ives is well provided with beaches and those at Carbis Bay and Porthgwidden are but a short distance.

Tate Gallery, St Ives

Foreshore, St Ives

St Ives

For hundreds of years pilchards and tin were the main providers for the working population of St Ives and most of the fishermen who survived on the former lived "Downalong" around the harbour, while those who worked the mines lived "Upalong". Both communities ultimately floundered the former with the disappearance of the pilchard and the latter with the collapse of the tin market. Happily however the town was discovered by artists – The Tate Gallery St Ives being the most recent legacy of this – and visited by the tourists who started arriving in ever increasing numbers with the extension of the railway to the town in the 1890s.

St Ives' Bay

The North

Godrevy Lighthouse
Cold and pale under heavy
clouds, iridescent and white
in the sun, thin yet proud as
a silhouette. Built in 1859, it
was the inspiration for
Virginia Woolf's novel *To
the Lighthouse.*

Hayle Estuary

Ever-changing according to the position of the sun and moon and thus the state of the tide. A long-established feeding ground for wild birds it is popular with autumn and winter waders, particularly godwits, curlews, and winter wildfowl.

**Pendarves wood
nature reserve**

Carn Brea
An Iron Age hill fort
surmounts the highest point
in the Camborne-Redruth
mining area at Carn Brea.
All around the 36 acre site
there are reminders of
Cornwall's more recent past
as the site is littered with
fragments of the area's
mining heritage.

Porthtowan

Porthtowan, cove of the sand dunes. Here, as one nineteenth century collection of folk-lore records, a voice was heard calling from the sea. Three times came the cry "The hour is come, but not the man", whereupon a dark figure appeared at the top of the hill, pausing just briefly before running down across the sand into the sea, never to be seen again.

Chapel Porth

A birds eye view of the National
Trust's idyllic Chapel Porth.
Unspoilt, natural, the perfect
valley entrance to the expansive
beach of this stretch of coast.

Perranporth

Today wave after wave of surfers head for the sands of Perranporth surfboard in hand. Fifteen hundred years ago, on this same stretch, St Piran arrived on the beach, with a millstone in his hands. The celebrated Celtic saint then settled here and the place has since been christened St Piran's port – Perranporth. Hailed as the Patron Saint of Cornwall, the ancient St Piran's Cross stands nearby in Perranzabuloe (from the Latin in sabulo – in the sand).

Wheal Coates

Scattered around Cornwall disused mine-shafts and engine houses are a familiar enough sight, particularly around Camborne and St Agnes and many of them known as Wheal ...

Wheal Coates

St Agnes

The 'Stippy Stappy' is a steep lane with steps of picturesque stone miners cottages tumbling down the wooded valley leading to the sea. St Agnes was made famous for its tin and proudly boasted that their's was the best in Cornwall. The village ceased mining in the early twentieth century and is now known as one of Cornwall's most unspoilt resorts.

**Dunes at
Perranporth**

Perranporth

Trevaunance Cove
Huge winter seas relentlessly erode this coast. There was once a small harbour here for shipping the ore from the cliffs tucked behind. The sea took its toll and the broken blocks lie strewn on the ocean bed. The beach is now popular with surfers.

Fistral Beach
The busiest surfing beach in
Cornwall is undoubtedly
Newquay's famous Fistral
Beach, a mecca for
devotees of the sport from
all over the world.

Newquay

Newquay is the largest resort on the north Cornish coast and has been ever since the railways started bringing carriage upon carriage of holidaymakers here, hence the fine Victorian hotels that still line the cliffs. The scene today is very much as Frederick Cowles described it in *The Magic of Cornwall* before the war in 1934; "Thousands of people were bathing, some were surf riding, and many family parties were playing cricket on the sands. Picnic parties were enjoying al-fresco meals, and ice-cream vendors seemed to be doing a good trade"

Windfarms

A relatively new feature on the Cornish landscape is the windfarm. First introduced here in the early 1990s this group of three-bladed power generators were imported from Denmark, where they have been producing electricity from windmills for over a hundred years. They appear vaguely surreal at the moment but seem destined to become more widespread.

Bridge at Newquay

Watergate Bay

A vast sandy expanse at low tide, Watergate Bay sits along a north easterly line from Newquay. A two-mile stretch of Cornish Coast Path follows the lofty cliffs at the back of the beach and offers spectacular views.

Watergate bay looking towards Griffin's Point

Looking further north along the coast beyond Watergate Bay we see Griffin's Point in the middle distance. There can be found another of the Duchy's Iron Age fortifications, with ramparts and ditches still clearly defined.

Bedruthan Steps

The area of coastline is now owned by the National Trust who have built a steep, yet secure, stairway down to the beach. The 'steps' are actually the rock stacks that jut out from the sea formed by the collapse of caves and arches. The 'steps' have been named locally as Queen Bess, Samaritan Island, and Diggory's Island.

Trevose Head

Five quite different and quite delightful beaches flank the Trevose Headland, Treyarnon, Constantine, Booby's, Mother Ivey's and Harlyn. This particular view of one of only two prime Mesolithic sites in North Cornwall is dominated by the great, white, mid-nineteenth century Trevose lighthouse.

Constantine

The rolling surf at Constantine and Booby's two neighbouring beaches does little to warn you of the strength of the under water rip of the former and the concealed rocks of the latter. When the appropriate flags are flying though both are extremely popular with surfers and bathers alike. The ruins of the fourteenth century church of St Constantine can be found in the golf course behind the beach.

Camel Estuary

A waterway at high tide, yet a vast expanse of sand twelve hours later, the Camel estuary is headed by the Doom Bar, a great sandbank said to have been created when a local mermaid threw sand and a curse at a man who attacked her. Many a boat has come to grief there since and the gradual silting up of the river over the years has made life difficult for commercial traffic but created a haven for wildlife, particularly the grebes, divers and winter wildfowl.

Wadebridge

Outstretched across the Camel at Wadebridge is the longest bridge in Cornwall. Widely regarded as one of the finest medieval bridges in England, it has seventeen arches and measures over 300 feet long. It was built in the middle of the fifteenth century at the expense of John Lovebond, vicar of Wadebridge's mother church of Egloshayle, and if Leland's story is true it was constructed on a foundation of wool packs. Hence the Bridge on Wool pub with its sign showing Parson Lovebond and his bishop over the newly completed crossing.

Padstow
Famous for its annual May Day 'Obby 'Oss (Hobby-horse) celebrations and luxury yachts, pleasure craft and fishing boats provide Padstow with a cosmopolitan air. The quaint diversity of the architectural styles, the building materials and the paint work of the properties that face onto the pretty little harbour combine to make this one of the most attractive of all of Cornwall's fishing villages.

Evening at Padstow Harbour

The Camel at Wadebridge

St Enodoc's Church

The small church is now placed in the middle of a golf course and the thirteenth century spire is only just visible. The structure is essentially Norman and built of Cornish granite. The churchyard is now most visited as the last resting place of the poet laureate John Betjeman.

Polzeath

The early evening sun casts long shadows across the flat sands of New Polzeath as a disparate horde of swimmers and surfers in their shiny black wet suits make the most of the waves. Known as Pentireglaze until 1972 when the popularity of the sea and the surf prompted the place to re-invent itself as New Polzeath – a twentieth century holiday town – it stands alongside old Polzeath. Water free at low tide, there is a vast expanse of sand across which the wind driven skeletal machines of land yachts regularly race while the more pedestrian visitors make a short cut across the beach as they tackle this stretch of the Cornish Coast Path.

Cottages, Port Isaac

Port Isaac

Port Isaac's thoroughfares are narrow, Sqeezibelly Alley is just eighteen inches wide in places. The pier here dates back to the reign of Henry VIII. At low tide, and at the discretion of one of the few remaining fishermen, it is possible to park on the sand of the harbour itself. Care must be taken though to leave some kind of path clear for the local Lifeboat, which in times of need still has to be manhandled down to the water.

**Putting to sea
from Port Isaac**

Quayside, Port Issac

Port Isaac

Bodmin Moor
Bodmin Moor's lower slopes gradually change from rough moorland to cultivated field systems. The landscape is scattered with Bronze Age hut circles and hugely imposing granite tors.

**Trees in a shower of rain
on Bodmin Moor**

Source of the Fowey

The sun confers a translucent light upon the leaves of the trees that sit at the source of one of Cornwall's major rivers – the Fowey. As a stream it rises here at the foot of the county's highest hill, Brown Willy, barely six or seven miles from the north coast of Cornwall. From there it meanders down through Bodmin Moor on its long journey south to the coastal town that proudly bears its name.

Launceston Castle

Launceston was once the capital of Cornwall and an important Norman stronghold. The castle still remains today and is managed by English Heritage. Although not all the motte and bailey structure remains its dominant position above the town reminds us of its strategic importance.

Dozemary Pool

High on Bodmin Moor sits Dozemary Pool. Here one thousand feet above sea level and more than one thousand years ago Sir Bedivere is supposed to have thrown Excalibur – King Arthur's sword. Twice, it was said, he hid it in the reeds, finally hurling it as his King had instructed into the deep dark waters, only to see a slender white arm rise out of the water and catch it. Long thought to be fathomless, legend also has it that for many years the restless spirit of Tregeagle tried to empty the pool with a limpet-shell – with a hole in it!

Bodmin Moor (right)

Brown Willy stands an impressive 1377 feet above sea level and boasts splendid views across this ancient landscape. Peppered with granite stone piles the moors can appear bleak and inhospitable to man or beast.

Colliford Lake

St Dennis Church
This church stands at 700 feet above sea level on the top of an iron age hillfort. The dedication may have originated in the Cornish word 'dinas' meaning fort. Its high vantage point gives it spectacular views across the china clay workings, slate roofed cottages and granite stone walls.

Cardinham Church

The church at Cardinham is dedicated to St Meubred and built of Cornish granite. In the churchyard stands one of the finest Cornish crosses in the county, reaching nearly nine feet in height it displays intricate scroll and plait work on its face.

Bodmin Gaol

A popular spot on the Camel Trail and you can generally expect to see cycles chained up outside. Part ruin, part pub, part museum today, Bodmin Gaol was the setting for a number of well attended public executions in the middle of the nineteenth century. During the First World War this foreboding complex was used to house some of the nation's most valuable possessions, including the Crown Jewels and the Domesday Book.

Cardinham Woods

Cornwall

Tintagel

We have Geoffrey of Monmouth, writing in 1147, to thank for focussing the core of the Arthurian legends here at Tintagel. Even now it is easy to see why visitors are seduced by this larger-than-life, fairy-tale, coastline castle. Whatever the true account of this place, it never fails to fuel the imagination.

First recorded as Tintagol in the middle of the twelfth century it was Tyntagel in 1233 when it was referred to as "Richards castle". The name Tintagel or 'din tagell', describes the place well, it is the 'fort of constriction', that is the defended place along from the narrow neck of land that separates the romantic promontory from the mainland.

Boscastle

A steeply set community with a tiny yet picturesque Elizabethan harbour, it is one of the few safe havens on a relatively long stretch of coastline. However, it is not the easiest to enter, the sea makes a double "s" bend and poses a challenge to the sailor.

Sunset on the north coast

Rock Pools, Widemouth Beach

Bude

From Bude southwards the coastline here is characterised by distinctive rocky outcrops of various shapes and sizes. Over millions of years erosion by the wind, rain and sea has blasted away much of the soft shale leaving uneven tracts of the more resistant sandstone and local limestone littered across the waterfront.

Bude

DUCHY COLLEGE
LIBRARY

© **1998 Mabecron Books Limited**
Text copyright © Mabecron Books Ltd

Photographs Copyright © Richard Strong

British Library Cataloguing in Publication Data
A card with the CIP Data is available from the Publishers

ISBN 0–9532156–0–1

All images were photographed using Mamiya 645 camera and lenses.
Film stock, Fuji, 50, 100, 400, 1S0.
Edited by Ron Johns, Rebecca Souster, Mabecron Books Ltd.
Design & typesetting by John Carden, 7 Cleveland Road,
Chichester, PO19 2HF
Origination by Peninsular Services (UK) Ltd., 17 Bartholomew Street,
Exeter, EX4 3BG
The Photographer and Publisher acknowledge the help given by Paul Rowell.
Mike North for film processing.
Printed and Bound by New Inter Litho Milan, Italy.